First published in Australia by HiveMind Productions LLC, 2020.

Copyright © HiveMind Productions, 2020.

Milly Taylor has asserted her moral right under the Copyright Act 1968, [2006], and Patents Act 1990, to be identified as the author of this work.

All rights reserved. No reproduction, copy or transmission of this publication may be made without written permission. No paragraph of this publication may be reproduced, copied or transmitted save with written permission or in accordance with the provisions of the Copyright Act 1968, [2006]. Any person who does any unauthorised act in relation to this publication may be liable to criminal prosecution and civil claims for damages.

ISBN: 978-0-6489108-9-3

Typeset/Cover Design by – HiveMind Productions.
Artwork – Kate Gillett   &   Milly Taylor Creative
@esthers.red.drum   @ millytaylorcreative

WARRIOR WOMYN
Arise from the Ashes

by

Milly Taylor

Artwork by:
Kate Gillett

Introduction

This is a journey of survival.

From the centre of my sorrow, battling with suicide, trauma, abuse, and mental health challenges. To the freedom and grace of stepping into my power.

This is a story of growth.

Through creative expression I was able to explore and reflect on the love, lessons, trials and tribulations of this life, as it poured from me in these words... and it showed me such great insight into the cycles that needed to stop before they killed me. Literally.

This is a victorious voyage of hope. Through fires and heartbreak...and home to myself again.

I lost the battle with suicide... but I won the gift of life!

This is a tale of the wild expedition to my happily ever after ... nothing was as I expected, but everything is perfectly what I needed.

I hope this journey inspires others in their own recovery to seek and find the exquisiteness amid the aching.

Keep going.

Life has a way of redirecting us to where we need to be, sometimes we just need to surrender and trust that what is meant for us is finding its way to us, as we find our way to IT… one small step at a time.

All we need to do is keep breathing, expressing, resting, connecting, loving, creating, believing and BEING… Choose life. Choose you.

For in every dark moment there is still your path, and your path requires your footsteps, and in every footstep of the warrior there is re-creation.

Always have the courage to rise again…. One. More. Time.

LIFELINE – 131114
Crisis Care - 1800 199 008
Suicide Call Back Service - 1300 659 467
Mental Health Emergency Response Line (MHERL) - 1300 555 788

Contents

My Womyn	1
My Men	2
Fire	3
Lovers	5
Games	6
A Dream	7
BE	11
Freedom	13
Narcissus	15
Thin Air	17
No. is a complete sentence	19
Anxiety	21
Vampire	23
Taking a Break	24
The Spell	25
RAGE	28
Save You	29
Stitches	31
Cheater	33
Shadow Womyn	35
Karma	37
Waves	39
Abandonment	40
Holly	42
Mother	43
Old Friends	45
Leila	47
Cycles	51

Know thyself to love thyself	53
Values	55
Walking through fire	58
Rose	59
Worth	61
Wolf Womyn	62
The Space Between	63
Song Sister	66
Permission	67
Feels	68
Calm Before the Storm	70
Forever in a moment	71
Breathe	73
Innocence	77
Into the Wild	79
Gaia is a Womyn too	81
Post Traumatic Growth	82
The Power	83
Rebel	85
True Womyn	86
Perfection	87
Pisces	88
The Artists	90
Creative Juices	92
The Storyteller	94
Song Circle	95
SHE	97
Goddess	98
Letter to self	99
Vows	101
Single on Purpose	103
Bloom	105

Let me be a Womyn	107
MINE	112
MONSTER	113
Goodbye Good Girl	115
Censor	118
Home	119
The Centre	121
These Hands	122
Yellow Brick Road	123
Lockdown 2020	124
WEB	125
Life Returns	128
Fierce Cunt	129
Victory	131

Milly Taylor

My Womyn

To the Warrior Womyn who inspire me,
the ones who hold me,
and allow me to hold them in return…
As we grow together and blossom
into new ways of being…
The cycles ever continuing their journey
with the moon and the tides,
as we rise together over and over again.
In this life and every life….

I am honoured to be you,
to know you and to raise you.
Stay fierce, yet soft and forever wild

Warrior Womyn

My Men

To the Warrior Men who have held me in safety,
the ones who have retold me that respect
is just the minimum,
and my worth is more than gold….
The true, healthy, masculine energies
that honour the feminine.

Who listen;
Who feel;
Who love;
Who stay.

The warriors who step up.
The warriors who pulled me up
from the battle ground of my sorrow
and reminded me that I have purpose
and that purpose is better,
when we stand side by side as equals.

Milly Taylor

Fire

I took my sight for granted.
Now I'm standing where you are
and the ocean doesn't make me feel as free.
In a thunder bolt of fire and flames
I landed where you are.
I saw you staring right back at me
All the fear it came to drown the feelings
as I danced for hell
and you danced to be with me in open flames.
How do I not feel it?
When it's written on my finger tips
to touch you like we'll never be the same

It feels like fire

Please know my heart is there.
Burn your way under my skin
Walk with me my love
Past these walls of fear
As we move on through a door,
we've never seen

Warrior Womyn

Into these arms, into these songs.
Into me and into you,
we are the fire in the darkness.
Touch me now
for I can't see another way through.

Stay awake my love.
We've been laying fast asleep,
but I feel it as we rise and fall.
This fire sets us free.

I will dance with you.
I will burn for you.

Within this raging storm of flames.

I need you now
Hold on somehow
In wildfire love
we are untamed.

Milly Taylor

Lovers

My heart tells me,
the moon and sun
are secret lovers.
Just like you and me.

In the dusk or the dawn
they caress like a mystery,
while poet's string words,
and string dreams

And the world, it will turn
as the traveller sleeps.
And neither lover will ever ask why.
They just shine in their time.

With pure faith they will share
once again, a love dance in the sky.

Games

Does it confront you
if I wear my heart on my sleeve?
Does it elate you
when my attentions disagree?
Who do you play with your
fierce resistance to yourself?
These games a tiresome,
tournament of love;
we try to quell....

Milly Taylor

A Dream

We sat in a cafe.
It was warm,
it was Fremantle.
"Oh!" he said,
"I have something to tell you!!"
He placed his hand on his third eye
and squinted as he pretended to forget…
"I…. ahhh…. hmmmm…."

His leg quivered,
in anticipation,
as he glanced around the room.
Searching for the words.

Finding only anxiety.

I smiled and waited patiently
I already knew
what he was going to say,
and I was amused by his nervousness.
He was *never* nervous.

We locked eyes.
He blushed.
"I love you" he said,
"I love you too babe"
…And my heart turned
into the sun.

Milly Taylor

~

You find me there in moments
when you let go;
when you surrender;
when you embrace,

Love.

Look straight at me
and marvel at this
joining of two hearts.
Drifting in the current together.

~

Warrior Womyn

~

Sometimes the way people treat you
says everything about their wounds,
and *nothing* about your worth.

Remember that.

~

Milly Taylor

BE

To put reason to expression,
it turns to stone.
From the water it was inside my body,
the blood I have let flow.
The surge of magick in my belly.
Emotion – oceans of it.

Turned to steel in your gaze.
Your need to reason
what should only ever be
marvelled and relished.

Man's need to elucidate
is what slays the balance
of mystery and poetry.
Teetering on a knifes edge.

Just look
…sometimes
Just feel

Now and then things happen
in this life for no other reason
than to show you there is beauty.
Resist the urge to limit
what is limitless.

Warrior Womyn

Witness it;
Hold it in your heart and mind.

Long for it.
Savour it.

Let it be,
a flash that finds behind your eyes
as you draw your last breath in this life
and you remember the moments
you just
let it
BE.

Milly Taylor

Freedom

There's freedom in a flower.
How it blossoms;
how it grows.

No one tells it how to open.
No one tells it where to go.

The clever stare in wonder,
while others walk on by.
And the flower,
held fast to the earth
just smiles up at the sky

It bends and moves
as wind does blow.
It relishes in rain;
it opens to the sunlight.
It is wild and free,
untamed.

It's quiet yet still realized.
No point to prove or say,
the flower it just blossoms there.
Every single day.

Warrior Womyn

And when the seasons pass over,
the flower bows its brow
and tucks herself in;
it's time to rest for now.

Until she buds anew again
and opens up to be.
There's freedom in a flower,
that I wish I felt in me.

Milly Taylor

Narcissus

How do you ask
to see my ways…?
And then lace your tongue
with malice;
as I step forward *to be seen.*

You are so mean
when your demons speak…
All in one breath
you summon me forward
and then cut me down;
so swiftly.

You do not want to see
'my ways'.
You want to see your reflection
in me.

The moments you love me the most,
are the moments that
I wear a mask…
just like yours.

Warrior Womyn

When I dance,
like you.
When I speak,
like you.
When I play the performer…
Put on the charm;
 just like you.

You do not want to see me.
You want me to become you.

Like Narcissus….
Your blind search
for your own reflection
will drown you.

Milly Taylor

Thin Air

Those moments when you are fire
and he declares you water.
A mother wound that cuts
at flesh as you try to repair
his aching abandonment,
with your staying power.

A father wound that makes excuses
for the way he likes
to make you feel invisible.
You stand tall, right in his sight,
but he likes you to feel small...
Even when you try
to be anything but small...

He looks right through you,
as if everything you are
made of has become thin air.
He breathes you in though
And life pulses through his veins
with the oxygen you feed him
by giving...
Constantly.

Warrior Womyn

Providing,
being there,
loving his lungs with every ounce
of your existence.
But still invisible you are…

If you left,
if only you left for a minute,
maybe he would feel
the void of you not being there…

The ache in his lungs without air
The slow of his heartbeat
when he can no longer breathe.
But you don't know
how to be anything…
but THERE.

Milly Taylor

No. is a complete sentence

Her **NO**
is enough.
Reason is a gift
that she does not owe you…

Your questions;
Your nuisance.
Entitlement to her space.

Her body;
Her heart.
You have no power here.

She said **NO**.
Take it and go.

Why hover in your privilege and toxicity
Pushing to diminish her power
with the looming
stench of misogyny.

Warrior Womyn

As if she must explain
herself and her choices
to a world that stripped her bare,
for generations.
To justify her statement to YOU;
one who knows nothing of her soul?

NO

You are here to groom your ego.
She is here to live
and breathe in peace.

She said **NO**.
And that is a complete sentence.

Milly Taylor

Anxiety

When your own thoughts
clasp your lips closed.
When your heart chokes
on your breath.

When sleep no longer finds you
in your weariness
and tears are the only thing
to leave your body willingly.
"Take it with you as you fall! Please!!!"

When every evil thing
that has or could ever happen…
Plays on repeat.

Your eyes are closed
but it's all you can see.
Trapped inside.

You lay silently,
in death-like stillness
so you don't wake him,
as he sleeps next to you.

Warrior Womyn

But, not even death,
will numb the pain
of these wounds within…
The words he said…

Your greatest daily triumph
is the smile that covers
this war being fought
within your body...

The bloodshed behind your grin...
Hidden...

Hold your tongue...
Hold yourself...

"Good Morning. How are you?"
"Yea! I'm ok!! How are you?"

Milly Taylor

Vampire

Let the night unfold
as loves heart moves.
Let it envelope dreams
of the young.

He will come to you
And your heart will sing,
with the words on the tip
of his tongue.

You will breathe him life;
he will take your soul.
Let him hypnotise you to sleep
with the love of an age.

No one sees him,
by day,
with his love,
that's so bitter and deep.

Taking a Break

You pulling away from me
was like tearing flesh from bones.

I cry over those bones
and wait for you return.
Bleeding out willingly
as I weep.
And the death moon rises
over winter.
Singing you home to my soul
like a crone.

I am so cold without you…

Milly Taylor

The Spell

I heard you say...
"Everybody leaves me
when things get tough"

So, I cast your name to my lips
irreplaceably.
Magick mantras;
prayers of promise.

Open and helplessly devoted
to rhapsodize your praise forever...
Even when your demons consumed me,
in the darkness,
I sung your name to the moon
so she would call you home...

I heard you say...
"Everybody leaves me
when things get tough"

Have you become one
of your own monsters now
my love?

...or was this the spell
you cast,
to make me stay?

Warrior Womyn

Milly Taylor

~

I wanted to die
so I sank breathlessly
into the winter waves
and awaited my fate…

I found myself fighting for life.
Maybe death is not desired
in this heart…
… But an ending to this pain…

~

Warrior Womyn

RAGE

Tearing ground
and screams of fire
breath
and
hatred.

There wouldn't be enough roars
in an army waging war
to rage you from me,
but I will roar you from me
just the same...

Milly Taylor

Save You

Those walls they were high.
You built them that way.
And you said you tried,
but you weren't happy.

Your demons they bite,
but I didn't sway.
Cause I thought my love
would save you some day.

All of your reasons;
they just don't feel true.
The roar of your demons;
you couldn't break through.

So, I sang till I was screaming.
Doing all I could do
so you would hear me.
Cause I believed in you.

We don't need to walk
through this life alone,
but all of that noise in you
wore us down to the bone.

Warrior Womyn

Now I don't feel lonely
stepping to the unknown,
I just feel lost now,
'cause you felt like home.

Those walls they were high.
You built them that way.
I can feel it's not right,
as your love falls away.

Your demons they bite,
but I didn't sway.
'cause I thought my love
would save you some day

I thought our love
would save you some day
I hope that love...
... Will save you some day.

Milly Taylor

Stitches

I felt you pulling stitches
as you sewed yourself to her.
The noose around my neck
tightened with every word you uttered
and your fabrications
became the only fabric
I could find warmth within.
I felt you as a saviour…

Even though it was you
who cut the cords
and watched me fall
away into oblivion.
You… You are a tailor of torment

Stories changed. Words,
 rearranged…
Fragments missing from wounds
and wombs.
Futures changed;
Forever.

Your masks altered so rapidly; I couldn't see your face
any more.
Hidden cuts on my coatings where the self-loathing
seeped from my body.
The words that held the knife
came from your mouth every time.
Your parade is so punishing…

Warrior Womyn

New stitches were made
from the love that I gave.
Stories told and unfolded.
Your final pull away,
like life from soul
in a swift tremble of finality
I wept over the tatters…
Picking through threads and deceits…
Finding sharp truths
that stuck in my fingers like pins…

… But I used those truths
to begin pulling stitches of my own,
to unpick the pockets
that you nipped and *criticised onto my skin*
they shed like autumn leaves…
And fell to the floor to die
with a love that was nothing but
a cloak of lies.

I saw them sway into the wind with a breath,
as I felt my heart let you go.
Stitch-by-stich. Away from a life
shrouded in deception,
masked for mendacities.
And now *I am naked in truth.*

Milly Taylor

Cheater

There are so many things
worse than death, my love...
... and may
every-single-one-of-them

find *you*.

Warrior Womyn

The lies you told:

      "I'm always *honest*"
      "She's *just a friend*"
      "It's all *in your head*"
      "I just need *time alone*"
      "There's *no one else*"
      "This *hurts me* too"
      ...
      "I love you"

The only truth I know:

      You are a liar.

~You were never worthy, of this heart.

Milly Taylor

Shadow Womyn

Does she know the names you called her?
When you lay within my bed?
To throw me from the scent of lies,
exuding from the things you said

You always were a faker
so, a faker's what you chose.
A lie is all you know to live
I guess someday she'll know,
My 'craziness',
was truth in pain.

"Oh babe, but it's all in your head…"
There's nothing but truth
as I learned your sleuth.
Now the warrior wants her bloodshed.
The darkness in you,
woke a darkness in me;
and you'll never see my light again.

For if you come near,
I will drown you in fear,
and skin you alive with this pain.
Murderous prowess.

Born of your lies;
A killer, The Don, The Demon.

At first, I was scared,
but shadow had purpose
as she stepped forward
from my dreaming.

She showed me to fight
within my own mind.
She held me as my wounds
found meaning
and we crushed every memory
and bathed in its blood.

Now I sleep to the sound
of you screaming…

Milly Taylor

Karma

To the fool who clawed
her way through the heart
of another Womyn,
to get at what she wanted.

You got what you deserved…
The man who let you do it.

Warrior Womyn

~

Tear him from me
more each day.
I do not want to feel him
anymore…

~

Milly Taylor

Waves

Little mermaid,
dive deep
with no fear.

You are the ocean
and he was a wave.
Part of you for a time
now dashed upon the shore.

Let go;
flow.

It was never meant to be forever.

Warrior Womyn

Abandonment

Never mind how
he abandoned you, my dear…
How did you abandon yourself
to be with him?

What is the most self-loving thing
you can do for yourself right now?

BE HERE
RIGHT NOW
WITH YOU

Be here in all the ways
he never was.
This is where it begins darling
WITHIN.

Milly Taylor

~

Self-care is everything...
and it all starts with

gratitude.

~

Warrior Womyn

Holly

Daughter of mine
you are most beautiful
when you are free…
Know this to the core
of your being.

There is no filter or fabric
that will ever be more exquisite
than the sight of you.

Your hair in the wind.
Your eyes to the sea.
Your feet on the earth.

                         And your heart,
open for the world.

Milly Taylor

Mother

A memory of soft hands,
safe hugs;
a freedom to explore
the jungle of my imagination.
Right there in my own back yard.

She taught me to write.
To harmonise a tune
and feel music with my whole body.
She is tender, like me,
but unbreakable and extraordinary
in every way.

A rebel and an adventurer
that found her way
from the coldest winter…
… to US
… sitting together at our piano,
side by side,
as rain drops fell outside
the window.

A tree house.
Home cooking
and flowers in the garden
placed by hands that know soil.

Warrior Womyn

She showed me how
to bloom through countless winters
by planting seeds of love.

Milly Taylor

Old Friends

There is something breathtaking
about old friends,
the ones who knew you then,
who know you now…

No matter the time or the distance,
you *see each other*…
And the walls
you didn't even know you'd built,
crumble to the ground.

You are seen…
for who you are,
who you were,
who you pretend to be…
Who you'll never be…
and you are loved unconditionally
– all of it – celebrated.

You feel them in your soul.
Like they never left…

Oh, how we've changed
and grown together
like wilderness and time…

Warrior Womyn

In my bones and soul,
like magick weaved
from ancestors' dances,
to the ground we stand upon
together now,
after all this time…

Milly Taylor

Leila

We've always looked
to the world in wonder.
What magick we have found there:

Black
White
Dark
Light.

All entwined in the tales
that drew us back together,
over and over,
like the moon and tides.

We flow and ebb.
We wax and wane.
Always coming back
to the centre of a mystic cycle.

Where you,
and I,
grow together.

Maiden to mother,
and some day to crones,
Wild Womyn as we move
between the worlds.

Warrior Womyn

My sister;
I see you.
In the blue – by my side
and as always,
we look to the world
in wonder.

Milly Taylor

Sometimes all you need
is sunsets, guitars
and good friends…

Warrior Womyn

~

When all feels lost,
return to the sea.
Let it remind you that
like you
all things ebb and flow.

And there is always beauty
and life
in the tides
as they rise and fall
with the moon.

~

Milly Taylor

Cycles

We move in cycles
from a centre point
of innocence
to wisdom.

Expanding and growing
with new colours
and shades between.

Always connected to the beginning
of who we were with our first breath
at the beginning of time itself.

We move in cycles;
From grandmother's womb
to grandmothers,
Mother,
Daughter,
Child.

Always connected to the beginning,
to the love that created our ancestors
– the love that created us.

Warrior Womyn

Always at our back
in our bones,
at our feet.
Watching and loving you
as you expand from a centre of innocence
– to the expansion of wisdom.

Passing on the love
to the new lives we bare;
always connected to the beginning…

Milly Taylor

Know thyself to love thyself

I am a mermaid;
A mystery.
I am deep and moving.
Peaceful and raging.
Whole on my own
and one with it all.
I am loving,
I am giving,
I am playful.
Still soft, yet fierce.

I am a day dreamer.
I play passive to keep peace.
I silence myself to satisfy others
and I forgive myself for that.
For I am ever growing
and changing with the seasons;
yet constant as a star.

A complete contradiction.
Never try to rationalise this rhyme…
You will die trying.

Warrior Womyn

I feel like a waterfall,
whether its love, hate, anger, laughter.
No half measures;
I overflow.

I am a creator,
stringing words into tapestries,
singing songs like webs
and blending turquoise like oceans…
as I ebb and flow in time and space.

I am a nurturer
to those who rest in my heart
and I am learning to offer
this same pleasure
to myself.

Fear turns me to stone,
but when I am safe,
I open up and overflow again…
I am afraid – but I am *so fucking brave*.

Milly Taylor

Values

I value deep connection,
vulnerability and a solid sense of safety,
unconditional love and freedom,
positivity and compassion.
I value realness.
I value wilderness.

I value the outcasts who are so
authentic that you don't have to
ooze the 'schmooze'
to be in their space.

The rebels.
The weirdos.
The lovers.
The Dreamers.

I want to be surrounded by these people.
To love and be loved by them
as we grow old together
drinking Gin and cussing…
… cackling at life
like old witches in the moonlight.

Warrior Womyn

I love real and raw and deep,
full of joy and pain,
bad jokes, stupid faces, dancing,
drunk on music, in the darkness,
floor boards and red wine.

Bare foot and salty
with twigs in my hair
and a song in my heart.

Meet me there or flight with your fear.
If I am not for you…
You are not for me.

Milly Taylor

~

The more realness you embrace...
The less fakers in your space...
                              Bye, Felicia.

~

Warrior Womyn

Walking through fire

Sometimes we have to walk through fire
to learn what we are truly made of.
It is through these experiences
that we find the magick we can conjure...

Ancestors passage through my veins
from fires of past eras;
through fire I have come
to embrace that magick and use it.
To be fierce when I breathe life into life.

To know I am worthy,
to know I am enough.

Milly Taylor

Rose

She is a rose;
soft like petals
and sharp when she bites.
She dies when cut
but blooms in radiant colour
when her roots touch naked earth…

Opening to sunshine,
fragrant in moonlight,
with a wild life of her own
and a romance about her when you hold
her softly with your fingertips…

Never to be owned,
but gifted, received and
appreciated for the smiles
she creates by simply being…

Witnessed.
Loved.
Remembered.

For the colour she brought
into the world in the spring…
And how it felt to stop time
and be with her

Warrior Womyn

… as you breathed her into your lungs
with life itself.

Milly Taylor

Worth

If you could see you,
through this heart of mine,
the adoration you give
to those who take and take and take;
would be shared with those
who give and give and give.

You are worthy!

Wolf Womyn

Your worth is not found
in the opinions of others.
Know that every time
you level up in life,
those who try to bring you down
and keep you small
have no right to be
a part of your pack.

Milly Taylor

The Space Between

The 'space between' is
all about self-discovery.
There is no need to rush
from one thing to the next….

Distracting.
Pretending.
Deflecting.
Replacing.
Denying.

All of these are forms of resistance
that simply perpetuate the wound cycle
and interfere
with the deep healing process.

Just BE.

This is how you remember who you are…
Once you remember who you are,
you know what to defend.

You find your own voice
again.
You hear your own heart
again…

Warrior Womyn

You build healthy boundaries
that you need to honour
that beloved soul of yours.

Milly Taylor

Sing,
when you are broken open.
This is how the light
gets in.

Song Sister

Birthing sound to
what was silenced;
poetry from pain.
Let it lift a soul that is weary,
as it's pouring out like rain.

Make it art.
Let it colour;
freedom to move.
Give it sound;
LET IT ROAR.
See, it's beautiful.

In creation,
we are unbound.
Someday, we move on
from painful states
and it all makes sense
in retrospect and truth
– the beauty of creative expression
is what's left behind when we do…

Milly Taylor

Permission

Matters of the heart
cannot be processed
with the mind.

You want to heal
your heart?

Give yourself permission to feel…

Feels

Cry it out.
Write it out.
Burn it.
Bury it.
Roar.
Breathe.
Draw symbols in the sand,
watch the waves wash it away.

Charge its energy
into the branch of a tree
and walk away
without looking back.

Drive it into fistfuls of sand
and throw it to the rivers
…. Tender heart.

You are feeling;
You are healing.

Milly Taylor

~

True love is *divine*
and so are *you*....

~

Warrior Womyn

Calm Before the Storm

Darkness on horizon.
The sound of silence here;
peace before the thunder
bristled knowing fear.

Diamonds on the water.
Sun peers through the clouds,
standing fated
anticipation.

Buried in the shrouds,
the calm before the storm.
It lights a peace in me
and I will be the centre
as it washes over me.

And I will find the axis
as I tread this ground
and I will stand connected.
To mother I am bound.

Milly Taylor

Forever in a moment

I remember you, lover.
When the walls were thin
and you slept in dream.
Straight nose,
dark lashes,
peaceful breathing;
I loved you there.

In the kitchen as you fumbled
over chopped vegetables
and furrowed your brow at recipes,
a terrible cook
with so many courses.

A laugh like your father,
lips like your daughter.
Strong hands;
Delicate things.
I loved you there too.

Watering concrete,
bathrobe, socks and thongs.
Planning a chess board
and gazing out to sea… Always thinking.

Warrior Womyn

Watching me,
watching whales on the horizon.
You were most beautiful to me
in the moments when no one
was watching you.

Your facades vanished and I saw
the essence of you;
captivated by numbers.
Lips moving
deep in thought
bodies like jigsaw pieces
cold feet on warm thighs.

Holding our hearts together
as we breathed with the waves…
Our mouths barely touching
as we shared the same air.

There, I will always love you.

Milly Taylor

Breathe

In this garden of the trees
something washes over me.
I am free.

In this heart beneath the veil,
here begins the Faerietale.
I am free.

Let it go, let it go.
Where you'll end up no one knows;
so, let it go

Let it run, let it run.
On your footsteps you've begun;
So, let it run.

And Breathe,
just breathe;
breathe

I love you,
I love you,
I love you,
I love.

We are all travellers here,
to this time, to this place.
From the earth we come, my friend.
To the earth we return one day.

                                So, Breathe,
                                just Breathe.

Milly Taylor

~

Lean in. That's where the growth is…

~

Warrior Womyn

~

What if your hearts' desire
exists on the other side
of your greatest fear?

~

Milly Taylor

Innocence

New love
light me,
in a dark place still healing.
Love grows
 deep rooted in a place
most vulnerable.

I loved you once,
before the world
had tarnished these hearts;
I see you now.

The man grown from the boy
I adored at the start
And we still love the same way
Like innocence and wilderness.

Play and sunshine.
Laughter and a belly full
of icy poles and summer heat;
There is no truer love than the first.
The love we felt, as children,
when the world was still
a safe place for us.

Warrior Womyn

Remember?
Old love
light me
in an old place still grieving,
breathing,
still believing.

That love grows
deep rooted
in a place most vulnerable;
innocence.

Milly Taylor

Into the Wild

Are you ready lover?
To roll like waves
into each other's gaze,
bubbling upwards for air,
yet down to the centre of the earth;
where souls entwine
and forever makes its mark
on everything that came before us?
I'll howl like the wilderness.
For nothing ever tamed
or destroyed me for long.
There is Warrior Womyn
in all the places I bleed.
I will leave you in rapture
as I hold you like you've never known
a Womyn to hold you before…
These eyes know truth.
This skin knows instinct.
This heart knows love.
This soul knows the way…

Follow me into the wild…

Warrior Womyn

A Womyn is an ocean;
Wild,
Deep,
Free,
Whole,
Open,
Moving,
Tempestuous,
Everlasting,
Undulating,
Restless,
Peaceful,
Vast,
Hypnotic,
Unruly,
Ferocious.

She was *never* yours to tame.

Milly Taylor

Gaia is a Womyn too

You crawl and glisten on her skin;
she's frozen but she's melting.
Will you deny her when she cries?
Will you survive her if she thrives?
Burning up, she wants to live.
All that you take she wants to give.
She'll hold you lightly with her bones.
A rage of thunder when she cums.
She knows you as you walk your path.
She's speaking to you from the heart.
A blade of grass a blade of steel.
A knife to spoke the turning wheel.
A warrior knows to behold her;
the fool in you tried to control her.
Mother, lover, goddess, earth,
water flowing, fire burn

From earth we come, to it return.

Warrior Womyn

Post Traumatic Growth

Every layer has purpose,
it's is all moving you deeper into truth;
illuminating the blessings.
Showing the growth journey, you have ventured...
...And the perfection that you have become
as you radically accept,
every layer,
with unconditional love
and compassion.

Milly Taylor

The Power

You're but a sword
in a king's great army
and I'm but a tear in the sea.
You disbelieve all
the science presented
but mortals and men we must be.

Your fear is growing
into your guard.
It's creeping through
cracks in your walls
and from atop this wall,
she's the king of the castle.

She is the King of them all.

Warriors stand in the eyes of our children.
As they march
to the drums for survival.
While you hide in spaces
and mask what you've taken
and turn the truth into your rival.

Warrior Womyn

Buried in the earth
are the little one's secrets.
Ear to the ground,
they do speak.
So, let your king wage war
on all of the people,
but the earth will pass on to the meek.
Time will be fleeting
to those in denial
and time will be hard
if you fear.
But for those who love and fight,
as we turn to day from night.

We will have a blessed hope
of dreaming here.

~for Greta
(Keep standing tall, Warrior Womyn)

Milly Taylor

Rebel

Feel the fear and do it anyway.
See the challenge and give it attitude;
you are stronger than you know

Warrior Womyn

True Womyn

A true Womyn is
an indestructible breath of wonder.
It's not about what rests
between those thighs baby.
It's about the gentle
yet raging gospel
of wild song that you gift this turning existence.

And the way you do it so
effortlessly,
when you stay true
to who you are...

Milly Taylor

Perfection

Creative *expression*
should never be solely about success…
…but about *expression*
Let it fly.
Create.

We were made to colour this world.

Perfectly imperfect;
Every shade,
Every key.
Throw the shame aside
and rebel against perfection
with the fire of your authenticity.
~~And~~ then charge into the world,
shaking colours and songs
wherever you go.
This is yours;
This life,
This heart,
This soul.
Give it permission to love out loud…

Pisces

Into the blue,
worlds turn,
and birth anew.
Where do you go
when silent ocean envelops you?

Immersed in the cool waters of home;
Salt,
Sea.
I am the oceans' daughter,
immersed in timeless verity.

Milly Taylor

~

You are *worthy* of the depths you give.

~

The Artists

There is music in these frozen woods.
Mysteries and sounds
from effervescent souls
bubbling up and out.
The skins of the creators
bristling in the silence;
this is how we breathe.
Taking in life,
breathing out poetry,
like trees,
like setting suns,
and rising moons.
Just waiting for that blessed moment
when hearts connect with art…
And we take your breath away for a moment,
filter it through our shapes
and colours and sounds and lyrics
and return it to you,
with pure love.

Creative Juices

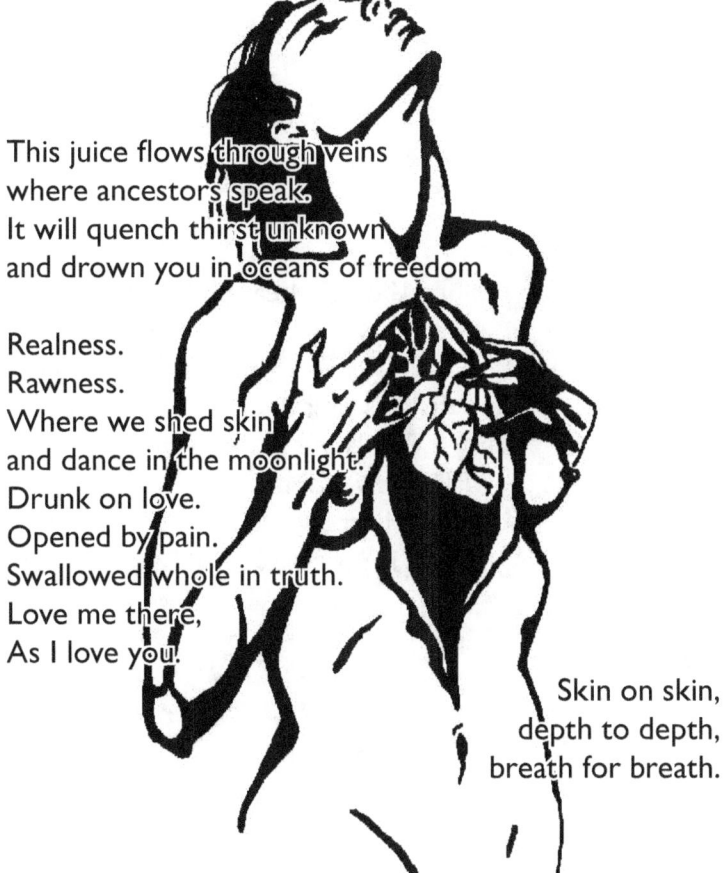

This juice flows through veins
where ancestors speak.
It will quench thirst unknown
and drown you in oceans of freedom.

Realness.
Rawness.
Where we shed skin
and dance in the moonlight.
Drunk on love.
Opened by pain.
Swallowed whole in truth.
Love me there,
As I love you!

                      Skin on skin,
                    depth to depth,
                  breath for breath.

Milly Taylor

~

It's all about making the pain beautiful somehow;

This is art.
This is music.
This is life.
This is wisdom.
This is growth.
This is purpose.

~

The Storyteller

Your colours paint this world
with the love and truth
of your adventures.

Breathe it in…

And then sing it out
for all the world to know.

Milly Taylor

Song Circle

Singing in circle with Womyn;
ancestral lines connected.
Daughter,
Me,
Mother,
Grandmother,
Great Grandmother,
And on, and on, and on.
A line of warriors roared
through me as I clawed
at ground where lives were born
and buried between my thighs…

Held by the greatest mother of them all,
who is neither good nor bad.
12 archetypes of sacred Womyn
running through 1 healer,
shattered and recreated
as I felt every rape,
beating, birth, loss, tear, triumph
and fierce rebellion roar
out of me into beauty.
Healed in space;
connected and turned over.

Warrior Womyn

As I rocked for the love of MY LIFE
and scattered old patterns
across a dancefloor
painted in my ancestors' blood.
Wild,
Free.
Vulnerable and fucking brave,
I saw her there in me.

The Warrior.
The Wife.
The Alchemist.
The Maiden.
The Mother.
The Crone.
The Priestess.
The Queen.
The Student.
The Maga.
The Teacher.
The Goddess.
The Wild Womyn.

And together we are so fucking strong…

Milly Taylor

SHE

Eye to eye.
Heart to heart.
She touched me lightly
in the place on my back
that makes me feel safe;
a heart sleeping, woke up
and loved.

She *witnessed* me,
as a wild animal
and danced in celebration.

At this untameable creature
she had woken in the dark.
Somehow it is she that waited in the wings,
to light the flame within.
Now her name tastes sweet
as my breath crosses my tongue
to speak of her.

She...
She...
She...

Goddess

A goddess walks within you, sister.
You stopped feeling her
when you tried to squeeze her
curves and edges, into reason.
Her wildness will never be tamed.
Let her hair free and barefoot rhythm
remind you of the dance of your own
ragingly beautiful heart.
Shake, Womyn, shake!
We don't conform
to society's norm.
We rage like fire,
flow like water.
With thighs and shoulders
bending on the horizon like undulating hills.
We were never made to be forever;
small… meek… timid.
Make noise and movement on the wild wind.
Break free.
Rebel against the ties within your own mind with a
blood fire war cry of "I AM ENOUGH"
Because you are.
And you always will be.

Milly Taylor

Letter to self

Dear one,
I love you just the way you are,
softness, fierceness, and *all*.
I was always here
and I always will be.
I'm on your side.
I believe in you.
I SEE YOU.
… And I love everything I find
Open up and let me love you…

Warrior Womyn

~

Magick happens when you choose
to love yourself.
It's a lifelong love affair
that will never let you down.

~

Milly Taylor

Vows

I will stand by my boundaries
I will be shamelessly
and authentically myself,
always, *in all ways.*
I will speak up;
I will do right.

I will follow the gentle pull
of my intuition and inner knowing.
I will live MY story.
I will honour *my* worth
and the life that I have created,
with so much love and passion.

I commit to creating
and allowing safety and adventure
in my world in every way…
Every day.

I will love myself as I am,
and only make space in my world
for those who do the same.
I will be gentle but fierce.
I will remain wild and wise.

Warrior Womyn

I marry myself to the moon and stars,
the earth and the ocean,
the mysteries of life
and the force that pulls us all.

- Love -

Blessed Be.

Milly Taylor

Single on Purpose

A hopeless romantic awaiting
her handsome prince?

FUCK THAT!

I am a Goddess who waits for no one……

Warrior Womyn

~

Love fiercely;
no half measures.

~

Milly Taylor

Bloom

Let your pain know purpose.
Let it grow into something new.
Honour it,
nurture it
and then… Bloom…

Warrior Womyn

~

It's a badass rebellion
to *love yourself*
in a world that capitalises
on your self-loathing.

~

Milly Taylor

Let me be a Womyn

Let me be a Womyn
known for her food.
Full bellies, empty plates
and satisfied souls,
will grace my life and my table…

Let me be a Womyn who plays…
I will drop the broom,
run through the mess
that can wait another day
and play outside in the sun…

Let me be a Womyn who writes.
Who strings words from
the *web of my soul*
and makes you melt
into the earth that you came from,
as the words hit depths you never knew existed.

Let me be a Womyn who sings.
Who haunts the breeze
with highs and lows
and takes you away on a melody

Warrior Womyn

Let me be a Womyn
who lives by the sea.
With sandy floors, hammocks,
trees and salty air.

Let me be a Womyn who is wild.
Naked in the moonlight,
bare feet in the dirt,
with the wind in my hair.

Let me be a Womyn who loves.
Who sheds my cloak
and dives willingly, but wisely,
into the waters of vulnerability,
deep, without fear.

Let me be a Womyn who knows.
Let me feel the past,
the present and future
and the faith that magick is always near…

Let me be a Womyn who dreams.
And, as age graces me day-by-day,
let those dreams blossom…
Another after another…

Let me be a Womyn who nurtures.
To love… To be home…
To be mother.

Milly Taylor

Let me be a Womyn who is fire!
Let my roar shake the rocks from the lost,
the hurt and the scared…
And when the armour does break
to the floor at their feet
Let our new skin shine light to one another,
let us be open, let us be bare…

Let me be a Womyn who dances.
Let the blood of my ancestors run
through me with every step.

Let me be a Womyn who is grateful.
I shall have what I love,
when I *love what I have*…

Let me be a Womyn who is open.
Let me cry the ocean within me
and dance in the rain
and when the raging sea
of my broken soul has calmed from the storm,
Let me create its story into a world of beauty,
music and colour.
Let me be a Womyn who loves herself.
Let me speak my truth,
respect my thoughts
and honour my being.

Warrior Womyn

Let me be a Womyn that opens her eyes.
On this day and every day,
to the magickal beauty that is
to be seen in everything.

Let me be an adventurer.
Let me shout 'YES' to life.
Let me be a conqueror.

I will rise again after every fight!
Let me be a lover.
Let me be a muse.
Let me be proud to be a wild confusion
and a complete contradiction.
Let me be loved for the free spirit in my soul
and the love I bare to this world.

Milly Taylor

Come to the depths of me,
without fear.
I knew you in your first breath
and I'll know you in your last.

Dive to the centre of truth;
I am here undefined.
I am not perfect.
I am not flawed.
Just vast, wide open and real
flowing currents and waves of change;
life giving, soul cleansing.
Darkness and light;
forever in a moment of blissful silence

As I wash you back,
to the epicentre of yourself,
with unconditional love every time you.

Breathe.
Dive.
Be.

I am waiting for you to remember you are home.

~Ocean

MINE

My body is mine.
My orgasm is mine.
My power is mine.
My heart, soul, life, breath…
It's all mine!
Treasures a plenty in the delight
that is me…
I now choose from a place of wholeness
who I allow in my space.

Honouring my body.
Honouring my soul.
Loving myself the way I have always wanted
to be loved.

I am mine.
I am mine.
I am mine.

That is where the true power is…

Milly Taylor

MONSTER

No more being hidden in the shadows.
I'm stepping forth into the light…
In my own right…
A life of wounds and stories.
Patterns that lead me to believe
that I'm a mother-fucking monster.
That my presence is offensive;
My blood, my voice, my body.
That I should be ashamed.
The cycle has ended.
I never needed your validation
or permission to BE.

FUCK YOU!

This monster is only a monster to those
who fear a Womyn in her power.
I know who I am now.
No longer hypnotised by your tales
and tall stories.
I know who you are.
Like a wolf in hunt, I see you so clearly,
I can smell your terror on the breeze
and taste your dread
in the dishonesties you speak.

Warrior Womyn

Your trepidation makes me blood thirsty,
for life.
Unadorned and untameable,
instincts sharpened by the years
you clutched my throat
and hid me in darkness;
fool.

I see you hiding behind your lies…
And so, I pulled your tendrils
from my soul
and left you there to die.

~Fuck the Patriarchy~

Milly Taylor

Goodbye Good Girl

I've played nice, saved face,
been passive and held back
for most of my life because,
I've placed my worth
in other people's value of me.

Being likeable took over being real.
Generations of Womyn
who have played the 'good girl'
passage through me,
as I heal the silenced voices
that whispered before me
for thousands of years…
And reconnect with the warriors
that who roared before them.

I. Am. DONE being a 'good girl'.
I've stepped out of the reticence
that strangled me for 37 years;
and people call me crazy.
Unable to stand the force and fire
that births as I flourish into my power.

Warrior Womyn

The truth is discomforting for some...
But I no longer care.
 For those who try to smother it
for the benefit of comfort and niceties.

I'd rather be crazy than quiet.
People will always try to shame
a Womyn who steps out of line...
Centuries of shame...
It's still the same.
I don't fucking care anymore.

Farewell to the 'good girl'
who stayed passive while lovers cheated,
mistreated, and lied.

Farewell to the 'good girl' who said 'yes'
or stayed mute,
when she should have said
"FUCK NO!".

Farewell to the 'good girl' who feared
BEING because society, family, lovers
and friends, said she was either
too much or not enough.

Milly Taylor

A new age of fierceness, authenticity,
joy,
truth,
self-worth,
peace,
compassion,
gratitude,
celebration,
and WILDNESS is born.

The ties are cut.
The spells are cast.
The ancestors are dancing
and the oppressors are retreating.
I've heard my voice
and I love her song;
I'll never silence my soul again.

Censor

I will not attenuate myself to appease you.
I will not censor myself.
I have a soul given purpose
that will never be accomplished
if I continue to bow to the oppressors
and their allies,
to those feeble attempts to diminish me
into silence and smallness.
I will continue to light like a beacon for others
until they can shine for themselves…
And others…
And so, the ripple continues.

This is how we change the world TOGETHER.
Step up!
Let your truth be a light in the dark.
Let your truth be a centre in the storm.
Let your truth filter those
who ebb and flow from your life.

Never censor yourself.
Never let them win.

Milly Taylor

Home

I wished to burn him from my skin
with the touch of another.
Somehow this body wasn't mine,
so, I am no one's lover.
Slowly seeping back to me
from fires and darkness hold
the centre of my pain within
with wisdom more than gold.

All of the intensity
was a big necessity
to bring all this truth to me,
to let those cycles go.
And somehow in this clarity,
truth is all I clearly to see
there's nothing left to do or be,
but feel this love, and grow.

Warrior Womyn

I know to hold this longing,
like a treasure trove.
For someday in the tides of time,
this moment's all I'll love.
Breathe it in survivor,
for every breath is sewn
to this body recreating,
as your coming home.

Milly Taylor

The Centre

Come back to the centre;
It's when eyes close
and earth magick breathes with you,
slowly…
It's there as music courses
through your cells
and onto your skin
and into your heart.
It's there as you touch the centre
of your sorrow
and your joy.
One
heartbeat
at
a
time.
It's there in silence
… And dreams…
It's there in you.
It's there in me.
Reach in
and be it…

Warrior Womyn

These Hands

Upon the tides
return to self.
Remember you're unbroken.
You bend,
not break.
To give and take,
so brave to remain open
to live and love,
to sing and speak.
To know the sound of truth
that blossomed in
your blessed skin.
The moment YOU held *you*.

Milly Taylor

Yellow Brick Road

In all the unkindness
and lost soul blindness that had
seeped through the cracks.
In her yellow brick road,
the magick and sparkle
of her own two feet;
the dance in her step.
The field of flowers where she slept.
The adventures never forgotten.
And friends who held her through…
She found her way home
with a wish;
a knowing.
That home was right where she started;
never parted.
It had been with her
the whole adventure,
holding fast to the part
that she loved the most.
A heart that *never stopped believing.*

Lockdown 2020

It's almost poetic justice when the world turns
 upon itself and thrusts you into solitude,
to bask in the home and inner worlds
that you had to turn upon
yourself to remember.

When you fall on your feet,
in the middle of mayhem.
When your solitude is heaven on earth.
When your home and heart
and family feel like shelter and contentment
and all this magicked into creation,
by *you*.

A place to be.
A place where tired bones
find themselves resting;
home.

You know you have done something very right.

Milly Taylor

WEB

The Womyn;
life of love and of earth.
Herbs and healing,
from the mother we birthed.
Wild and knowing,
shadow chase over the bones
of what's past,
to lay down what's yet to come.
The witches
death of blood and of fire.
The lost ones,
confused with their lost desires.
RISE UP.

Walked in peace into the sea;
many sacred.
Flow in oceans of the free
they weaved a web of knowing
they weaved a web of love,
they weaved a web for the old ones
and they weaved a web for us…

Warrior Womyn

The mothers;
birthing tears and a child.
And the lovers
Womyn powerful and wild.
Heart of Womyn;
heart of nurturing all.
Weave the web
from the strings of your soul;
and you weave
a web of knowing;
and you weave
a web of love;
and you weave
a web for the old ones;
and you weave
a web for us.

Milly Taylor

~

And so, THIS is safety.
That yearning and emptiness
consumed self-loathing
that I placed inside myself,
like a fabricated imposter
it wasn't real.
Safety was here within these walls
of my skin all along.
This space where I am loved unconditionally
celebrated for who I am,
here,
all along.
I just needed to empty the space
to clear my vision,
to open the portal…
So that I could fall into it;
through the layers,
through the heartaches,
through the stories,
through the unknown.
To land here…
In me.
The safest place in the world.

~

Warrior Womyn

Life Returns

Solitude shows us that life
returns in stillness.
The waterways clear.
The dolphins return.
The wild elephants sleep in the field
and the birds sing songs
that can finally be heard
on the gentle winds of time.

It is here that we remember
we have the power,
to celebrate the small things.
It is here that we create.
It is here that we connect.
When we slow down,
we remember who we are…

Milly Taylor

Fierce Cunt

Slut – they called you as you took your body
 back from them and claimed
your sexual pleasure as your own.
CRAZY! They branded you
when your truths burst their lies into flames.
Crass, they said,
when you unapologetically spoke actuality,
that they couldn't accept
– in a world that told you
to remain meek to be a
'satisfactory human'.

HOW DARE YOU!

Aggressive – they will say,
when you stand for what you believe in
with conviction.
BITCH – they will slander,
every time you say NO!
Bossy, they will declare,
when you give direction without hesitation.
Oversensitive, they'll dismiss,
EVERY time you feel.

Warrior Womyn

Instigator – is the brand of a Womyn
who stirs their discomfort
in all the right ways.
INCORRIGABLE are the girls
who burst free from the binds
and stamp them into the soil
with their naked dance.
unbound by conformity and refusing
to break their limbs from limbs
to FIT IN.

FREEDOM!

When the world drums a beat
that repeats that you are 'too much'
or 'not enough' in an attempt to weaken,
your untameable spirit.

Move to your own damn rhythm.

… And keep being a fierce cunt.

Milly Taylor

Victory

The roar of a freed wild Womyn
is a beautiful thing.
It rises from her womb
and claws through a heart once shattered.

Crosses lips
no longer bound by untruths
and breaks the horizon
as darkness swallow's day.
She dances in the shadows knowing
Although you tried to silence her.

You will never win.

Welcome home wild one…

~ *Warrior Womyn*

www.ingramcontent.com/pod-product-compliance
Lightning Source LLC
Chambersburg PA
CBHW070307010526
44107CB00056B/2516